THE GHOSTLY TALES OF SAN DIEGO

Published by Arcadia Children's Books
A Division of Arcadia Publishing
Charleston, SC
www.arcadiapublishing.com

Spooky America is a trademark of Arcadia Publishing, Inc.

First published 2022

Manufactured in the United States

ISBN 978-1-4671-9882-0

Library of Congress Control Number: 2022933026

All images used courtesy of Shutterstock.com; p. 30 S and S Imaging/
Shutterstock.com; p. 72 Manuela Durson/Shutterstock.com; p. 86 achinthamb/
Shutterstock.com.

Notice: The information in this book is true and complete to the best of our
knowledge. It is offered without guarantee on the part of the author or Arcadia
Publishing. The author and Arcadia Publishing disclaim all liability in connection with
the use of this book.

THE
GHOSTLY TALES
OF
SAN DIEGO

SELENA FRAGASSI

Adapted from *Haunted Heart of San Diego* by Brian Clune with Bob Davis

NEVADA

UTAH

CALIFORNIA

ARIZONA

PACIFIC
OCEAN

SAN DIEGO

Table of Contents & Map Key

Introduction

San Diego is often called "America's Finest City." After all, there are few other places in the fifty United States where you can find picture-perfect sandy beaches and surfer waves that stretch for miles, a sky that always looks like it's painted blue, and the best weather—around 74 degrees all year.

But, for all its beautiful views, there is something a bit darker beneath the surface of San Diego—it's the place where the spirits of the past stick around and sometimes still make appearances. You see, San Diego is where California was born, meaning it's quite an old city and with it comes a rich history that isn't ready to go away just yet.

It's also a city that wants to make sure its famous spots from centuries ago are kept up, from old Navy ships and lighthouses to the many saloons, stores, and hotels. And yes, those who once visited and lived in these places still seem to hang around and "mingle" with those who visit today. So let's begin our journey to this spooky coastal city and see what lurks under and above the water.

Casa de Estudillo

Casa de Estudillo

Welcome to the area known as Old Town San Diego. It's called "Old Town" because it's where people originally lived—as early as 1769. This was before California became the thirty-first state in the US and San Diego became its first city, both of which happened in 1850.

This moment was a long-time coming. A Native American tribe called the Kumeyaay had lived in this region for thousands of years. Then

Spanish explorers arrived in the 1500s and 1600s, claiming a huge area of land for Spain, including what is today California, Mexico, and more. In the early 1800s, the Mexican people fought the Spanish to control California, and won. The US did not gain control of the area where San Diego now lies until the late 1840s.

San Diego itself, however, had started coming together in the early 1800s. Many of the buildings had a Mexican or Spanish style. This is what still exists in Old Town today with many of those structures still standing. The city works hard to keep the buildings safe and beautiful. Even today, many travelers still love to visit these sites.

One of those buildings is the Casa de Estudillo. It was first built by a war general, José Maria Estudillo in 1827. Unfortunately, he died three years later and never got to live in it. His son (also named José) finished the construction. It had a very interesting shape that was popular back then. It looked like the letter *U*. (If you can picture it, it was long on each side with a shorter piece connecting them in the center.)

The whole property was very large—there were twelve separate rooms, plus a big kitchen and chapel. The Estudillos were a very wealthy family, and they owned a lot of land where they had farms and made wine. They could afford to build a property this big, but the Casa wasn't just for them. It was for everyone in town! A priest also lived there. Others were invited to come and hold mass in the chapel for anyone in town since there was no other church nearby. The Casa also was used as a schoolhouse during the day—students would learn in a large room that the Estudillo family then used as a living room. So much more than a Casa, it was a community center for all of San Diego.

But then something weird happened. A book was written in 1884 by a woman named Helen Hunt Jackson. It was called *Ramona* and it became very popular. It was set in southern California, the same area as San Diego, and many people started coming to town wanting to see all the places mentioned in the book. For some reason, the local newspaper, the *San Diego Union,* wrote an article that said that the Casa de Estudillo was the house where the book's main character Ramona got married. It wasn't true, but it didn't stop tourists from showing up to the Casa wanting to see inside.

When this started happening, the Estudillo family was not living there—they had moved to Los Angeles. But a person they put in charge of the property had an idea: they started taking apart the house and selling pieces as *Ramona* collector's items. As you might imagine, this destroyed the Casa and it was left torn apart— even the walls were sold to fans of the book!

The Estudillos decided they could do nothing more with the property, and it was sold. The Casa remained a popular tourist attraction for many decades, with even a gift shop added on later. That was until 1968 when it was sold to the state of California. Today, the Casa is a museum. But visitors have experienced some frightening things, and many have said it's one of the most haunted houses in San Diego.

The first occurrences go back to when the house was once being remodeled. It's said that some of the workers noticed their tools went missing or they'd hear knocking on doors when no one was there. Tourists have also experienced strange events. Even today, many swear they can smell fresh bread baking and want to buy some to take home. And although there is an oven outside the Casa where the smells seem to come from, it hasn't worked in a long time. It's impossible for anything to bake inside of it.

Also outside the Casa, there have been strange occurrences surrounding a well. When looking into the deep, dark pit of the well, many said they have seen a set of eyes staring back at them. It all started with a bride who was posing for pictures next to it—she fainted when she saw someone looking at her! Ever since that time, the same thing has happened to many visitors, some who even swear there's a person trapped inside asking for help. But no person has ever fallen in. It happened so much that they eventually sealed the well shut.

Inside Casa de Estudillo, things are even spookier. Here, doors and windows slam shut as people walk by, even though there's no one there and no wind that comes through with that kind of force. Some have even said objects in rooms were "thrown" at them, or they have seen figures appear in mirrors or have heard voices telling them to "get out."

Some of the most spine-tingling moments occur with spirits of people. There is a priest who is seen roaming the grounds near the chapel, gardens, even the kitchen. When he sees you, it's said he holds up his hand like he's giving a prayer, smiles, and then vanishes into thin air. A Mexican cowboy who some say might have been one of the Estudillo family's workers has also been spotted sitting in the dining room—he walks to the table, sits down and then is gone like he never existed. There's also a little girl dressed in old-time clothing who likes to hang around in the bedrooms and sit and sway back and forth in a rocking chair.

No one is quite sure why there are so many ghostly adventures at the Casa de Estudillo since it was such a happy place loved by many

in the early days of San Diego. There were no sad deaths or accidents that happened inside like in other haunted houses. Though it could be that family members, former workers, and others who loved the home as their own want to make sure it's still doing okay after all the changes it's gone through. Maybe they're just watching over the Casa as its guardian angels.

Old Town San Diego

The Haunted Shops of Old Town

You'd have to look really hard to find another place in the country that has all the unique types of shops that exist in San Diego's Old Town neighborhood. There are retro candy stores, tobacco shops, and even places to buy rare gems and stones. But those making a visit might get more than they pay for. They may find some mystery shoppers lurking near them who took the idea of "shop 'til you drop" a bit too seriously!

Racine & Laramie Tobacconist is one great example. This store sells pipes and cigars, though one can never tell if all the smoke is coming from those items or maybe from the ghosts that haunt the shop. The building was one of the very first in Old Town and was originally the home of a man named Juan Rodriguez. Juan was what was called a "Leather-Jacket Soldier" back in the 1820s—named that for the jackets they wore to protect themselves from arrows during battles with Native American peoples. After Juan passed away, his family decided to let the tobacco shop rent the building. There was a big fire in 1872 that burned it to the ground, but in later years, experts built it back up again.

Today, Racine & Laramie still sells items for smokers. The shop looks just like it did back in the good old days. It also feels like that for the people who have been sticking around.

One ghost that everyone seems to meet is a little boy named Philip. He was one of Juan's family members who sadly died inside the building in the 1850s from a disease called smallpox. He makes himself known by playing funny pranks on people. Sometimes, Philip likes to slam the back door shut without warning, or he might spy on customers from the upstairs balcony. If he's caught, he might stick his tongue out and then disappear, though his giggles can still be heard after he leaves. Another spirit at the shop is a beautiful young woman named Kate. Not much is known about her except that she may have been meeting a man secretly at the hotel, which was once next door to Racine & Laramie. It's believed that when the secret was discovered, Kate was attacked by a person with a knife and then fell to her death down the back stairs of the building. Sometimes a loud thump can be heard outside, which could be Kate sadly reliving her last moments.

Of course, you might expect a bookstore to have some great ghost stories, and Captain Fitch's Mercantile does not disappoint. It's located in what used to be Old Town San Diego's first post office. After it shut down, the building sat empty for years collecting dust and quite possibly lots of lost spirits— until Captain Fitch's moved in. It's the only bookstore on this side of town, and it even sells lots of books about hauntings! The store is named for a local seaman named Henry Delano Fitch, who some believe is one of the ghosts

still making himself at home here. One of the things he likes to do is to move books around or throw them on the floor, which employees are not too happy about when they arrive for work each day and have to clean up his mess. Even during the middle of the workday, Henry will toss more books, even after the staff has just put them back on display. Sometimes customers will ask if something is wrong with the shelves since they can't get things to stay on them. Maybe Henry just wants someone to listen to his own story?

If you've ever been to a rock and crystal shop, you might have sensed something . . . otherworldly about it. Many people believe that rocks and minerals are mystical. Often, people who have psychic abilities and work with spirits will buy them. Miner's Gem Shop in Old Town has an energy just like this. In fact, the owner believes the spirit of a woman named Maria (who used to live in the family house that was once here) likes to hang around, even after closing hours. Maria is very much a night owl and, when the shopkeeper is ready to lock the doors and go home for the night, he can hear noises even though no one is inside. Maria also likes to make appearances on the security camera set up in the back of the store. The owner knows Maria is there when he sees an unexplainable black bar quickly move across the screen. Some might call a person who is so dedicated to keeping the store safe an employee of the month!

Before leaving Old Town San Diego, many people like to stop by Cousin's Candy Shop to get a treat. The building used to be a place to buy items for horses—like saddles and brushes—but today it sells classic goodies and candy, like saltwater taffy and licorice.

The spirit that haunts Cousin's seems to be pretty greedy however, and wants to keep all the candy! They love sugar so much that sometimes they can be heard talking about their favorite kinds of treats, and other times the candy scoops mysteriously fall to the floor. But really, who can blame them—loving candy doesn't just stop after you pass away!

CHAPTER 3

Cosmopolitan Hotel

If you've ever stayed overnight at a hotel, you know a lot of people pass through the lobby day and night on their way to their room for a good night's sleep. In fact, many hotels have hundreds of individual guest rooms, meaning *thousands* of people will stay in the building over the course of time, each with their own stories. The walls can feel like they are alive with these tales, nearly bursting with all the energy. San Diego's Cosmopolitan Hotel is no different.

When it was built in the late 1820s, the Cosmopolitan Hotel was the home of a man named Juan Bandini. Originally born in Peru and raised in Europe, he moved to San Diego in the early days of the town with his retired father. Juan had earned lots of money as part of a family of famous sea captains, and later became an important politician with his own cattle ranch. In fact, he helped the US gain the land that is now California during the Mexican-American War. He was very well known and respected and he wanted to build a house that fit for a king.

Juan's first wife was a woman from the Estudillo family (the same family that built the big Casa de Estudillo from a couple chapters ago). Like them, Juan received a big plot of land and he also wanted to build a U-shaped property like they had. His house, though, was raised up from the ground, so it stood even taller, like it was on a throne. It had fourteen bedrooms, a massive dining room (where he hosted large feasts), and a large wood floor that was used for dance parties after the feasts. It also had a beautiful clay tiled roof that made it stand out—so much so it was considered the biggest mansion in America at the time.

Though the Bandini family often held lavish gatherings and invited anyone from the community to attend, the good times did not last long. At the time, Mexico still owned the land (this was before California became an official US state). There were still Native American tribes trying to claim the area, so conflict was constant, and all of it left Juan broke. He lost many of the animals and crops on his ranch, and he started selling his valuables just to have food to feed his family.

One of the valuables was his large home, which he signed over to his son-in-law just a few months before Juan passed away in 1859. Maybe as a response to its owner's passing, the house also started to experience a slow death as its walls literally crumbled from lack of care as well as earthquakes and windstorms that became frequent in the area.

A decade later, a new buyer came forward who completely remodeled Juan's house back to its former glory. His name was Albert Seeley—he was a Texan who worked as a stagecoach driver (like an Uber back in the day that transported passengers, sometimes over long distances). He thought of using the house like a fancy hotel for his clients on their travels.

In addition to adding a second story with a balcony, a lobby, and some space for stores on the lower level, he put a fresh new sign on the roof that read "Cosmopolitan Hotel."

As well as being a hotel, the building also housed a post office, barbershop, and a few other businesses. Because it wasn't really the fanciest place to stay like Albert hoped it to be—the beds had straw blankets and there was no running water in the small rooms!—it wasn't exactly the place many out-of-towners chose. Instead, local people used it mostly for weddings and other events that could get kind of rowdy. But that business eventually stopped too as railroads came to the town and drew people to other close cities like Los Angeles. From that time forward the Cosmopolitan Hotel had a few different lives, first as a boarding school, then as apartments during World War II, and then a South American restaurant with office spaces before the year 2000.

Then, in 2005, the State of California invested money to turn it back to a beautiful, updated version of the Cosmopolitan Hotel, again giving the building its same name. Today it welcomes guests and many people come, either wanting to see a piece of history—or to get some good ghost activity. It's believed that Juan Bandini still enjoys all the rooms in the house he built. In fact, ghost hunters have captured him on voice recordings using special equipment.

Another spirit said to be lurking around is his daughter Ysidor. She especially loves Room 11. Many people like to request that room for their stay, and they sure do get the scary experiences they are hoping for—she really enjoys playing with the lights, shutting them off when someone might be in the shower or getting dressed with no way to turn them back on quickly. Or they can flicker off and on rapidly, sending shivers down people's spines. Ysidor likes to move things around in the room too just in case anyone doubted she was there. Sometimes it's a shirt that falls off its hanger or pens that randomly move across the desk.

Room 4 also has an unexpected guest—very unexpected. In this room the bed has a headboard and a dresser both carved with the image of a little girl—and she sometimes appears to come to life! As the story goes, the man who crafted these old pieces of furniture was grieving the death of his young daughter and the grief may have been too much for the girl who is likely still looking for her father. She may have friends there, too, as sometimes the sound of children laughing and playing can be heard in various corners of the hotel even though none are there.

El Campo Santo Cemetery

CHAPTER 4

El Campo Santo Cemetery

When people pass away, they are often buried in cemeteries where loved ones have the chance to come and visit, keeping their memories alive. It happens sometimes that cemeteries are moved to make way for a new building or roadway. When this happens, the coffins and remains of the deceased need to be moved to new plots of land. It's a big task! And it is the respectful thing to do. In some cases, however, to save money or to save the effort, bodies can be left behind while the new buildings go up right on top of their resting places. And you can imagine this does not make spirits happy!

This is exactly what happened at El Campo Santo Cemetery in San Diego's Old Town. The name translates to "Sacred Ground" and the spooky stories that have come from this spot surely make that name ring true. El Campo Santo was first set up in 1849 and, over the course of a few decades, almost 500 people were laid to rest here.

But in 1889, the growing town of San Diego

was installing more horse-drawn streetcar lines to take residents back and forth from their homes to jobs and stores. Part of the rail tracks were planned to run right through the cemetery—and although the developers said they would move the twenty or so bodies that were in the direct path to a new area in the cemetery, they lied and only moved the headstones. This made it look like they completed the job even though they knew the bodies were still underneath the new streetcar tracks.

Not only that, but as time went on and streetcars went out of style, the bodies were

again disrespected when paved roads were built on top. Can you imagine hearing constant screeching brakes and car horns as you tried to rest in eternity?

By 1993, these poor souls were finally discovered using special tools that could sense their presence underground—but they were so far down below the surface of the town at this point, that all that could be done was to put a little grave marker in the street or sidewalk. Even worse, no records are left so the names of those who died are unknown. All that's written on these little markers are the words "grave site," almost as if the people never existed.

As you can imagine, all that unrest and sadness of being forgotten has caused a lot of ghostly activity in this part of town, a part called Old Town Village. Houses in the area experience the power going out or kitchen stoves and refrigerators not working for unexplained reasons. Some have even heard loud alarms blaring with no explanation. People who park in front of the cemetery find that they can't start up their engines when they want to leave—and after calling a tow truck to help rescue them, the service person finds absolutely nothing wrong with the car.

Inside the cemetery gates, there are a few interesting characters that roam and look very out of place, too. One is a Native American man with a big headdress strolling along not noticing anyone around him as well as a lady

in old-fashioned clothing. She will sometimes turn and smile and then seem to disappear back into her grave.

One of the known residents of El Campo Santo Cemetery is a man named Antonio Garra, a chief of a Native American tribe who once waged war and paid a heavy price for doing so. He was sentenced to death by a firing squad, and it took place right over his gravesite so that after he was shot, his body would fall right

in. Today he can sometimes be seen inside the grounds or on the rooftops of the houses that now surround the cemetery and sometimes he even appears *in* the houses or other nearby stores. If he's not seen, then it's sounds that tell of Antonio being in the area, like war cries or gunshots that ring out. After all, if those buried at El Campo Santo can't be at rest, then neither can the people living near there today.

CHAPTER 5

Haunted Village Restaurants and The Old Town Saloon

Dining out near El Campo Santo Cemetery also presents some very unexpected guests that sometimes want to join the table for a good meal. They especially seem to love Mexican food. Tahona Mezcaleria is one place where the former "locals" like to go—this small spot has one ghost that likes to play pranks on people using the restrooms after a night of tacos, chips, and guacamole. After someone closes the door to use the bathroom, they'll hear a knock at the door followed by a voice that says they really need to go—but as the person inside the restroom hurries up, they'll exit to find no one at all waiting to use it.

This ghost may or may not be the same spirit as one named Gregorio who is also up to a lot of tricks. No one really knows his story or his real name, but they can always feel him hanging around the restaurant—especially when they can't find items they need like kitchen tools or dishes. When they go looking for these necessary pieces, they won't be able to find them anywhere—and then like magic, when they come into work the next day, suddenly the forks and knives and everything else will be right back where they belong. Gregorio might have been the same mischievous person when he was alive, and maybe he's just bored trying to figure out what to do in eternity. Either way, it just seems he wants to have fun and isn't hanging around Tahona to disturb anyone.

Another popular place to eat near the cemetery is Fred's Mexican Restaurant, though the ghost that lingers here is one that staff are more likely to see than diners. In fact, the manager Ray likes to bring it up during interviews with new workers to see if they will be a good fit before they are hired. The ghost here likes to stay in the creepiest place of all, the restaurant's basement.

The employees think she may be a little girl, around seven- to ten-years-old, and she really likes to surprise people by slamming doors shut when they're heading down to the basement to pick up some supplies. With no open windows or air conditioners down in that level, there's no real explanation for how a door could be closed so roughly, and it unsettles workers every time—in fact, no one ever likes to go down there alone. The staff once even held a ritual inside the restaurant with incense, trying to clear out any unexplained energy, but there are still some occurrences. One time, one of the bartenders went downstairs to grab some more bottles, and swears he saw the body of only half a man standing before him. He could only see from the man's stomach up and it appeared like he had no legs. It was unlike anything he'd ever seen!

Finally, Café Coyote is one more restaurant where a lot of unusual activity is said to take place. Probably because it's built right on top of where the old El Campo Santo Cemetery used to be. The kitchen here is where many strange things happen, like cooks hearing whispers in their ear (maybe telling them to add more salt?) and finding pots and pans missing. There are even times when they're cooking meals and the stove turns off by itself! And at night, when the workers are cleaning up after the last guests have left, they can see faint images of children chasing each other and knocking into the tables and chairs. In real life it might make an adult tell them to stop it but seeing them so ghostly usually leaves people stunned and silent.

A fun night out at the bar with friends can often produce lots of stories that are retold for years, especially for those visiting the very popular Old Town Saloon in San Diego. If you visit here, your stories might include that time you took a seat at the bar and ordered a beer only to feel an unfamiliar hand trying to grab it away from you!

There have been many interesting occurrences over the years, since Café Coyote first opened as a mechanic shop in the 1920s or 1930s. It was built over a part of the El

Campo Santo Cemetery that no longer exists so spirits still seem to be "trapped" and make their presence known. In fact, sometimes when buried bones are found (like when a new building is constructed and the crew digs deep into the earth and finds the remains), power will go out in the whole neighborhood. It's as if the spirit is finally celebrating being freed and wants people to know about it in a very dramatic way.

Today the saloon, which still has that kind of look you might see in a Western cowboy movie, is owned by a family who has a lot of tales of ghostly experiences. There was a time they still had those old-fashioned swinging doors you see in the movies when a duel is about to happen between the good guys and bad guys. When people entered the saloon, they'd have to pass through these doors, which would naturally pause as the person walked through before swinging back and close again. Which is all fine and good, unless you're bartending and see that same motion happen and no person passes through! This has happened many times to people working, with no explanation—and even scarier, at the same time this occurs, an image of a person will appear in the mirror behind the bar even though there is no one there. The mirrors had to be removed because it scared people too much.

Even with the mirrors gone, however, bar staff and guests both still report being touched every now and then, especially if they are hanging out in the back of the saloon by the pool tables. Some say they have felt an arm around their waist like they are being weirdly hugged and some may feel like they are being pushed—which certainly doesn't help them line up the right shot in their game of pool!

Another spot in the saloon where ghosts like to mess around with people is the bathroom, just like at the Tahona Mezcaleria. It must be a popular place for the afterlife! The saloon was recently remodeled and the back part of the building—which used to be a barbershop—is now large restroom facilities with a big storage closet. Sometimes when people are doing their business, they'll feel and see footsteps in the bathroom with them even though they are the only one inside. Or the lights will flicker as they're washing their hands. Whoever is haunting the bathroom is also very fond of keys as he or she likes to steal them. The keys will eventually reappear but it might take days. Some of the bartenders have even had to call their husbands and wives to pick them up after work.

The current owner of the bar thinks his father may be one of the ghosts. His dad bought the bar in 1976 and has since passed away but might not be ready to fully say goodbye to it yet. Sometimes when his son comes in to work for the day, he'll smell cigarettes like his dad used to smoke (even though the state of California doesn't allow smoking inside bars and restaurants). Or, some believe, one of the ghosts could be good old Thomas Whaley who owned the very haunted Whaley House that still sits across the street—after all, the saloon is known to be a favorite spot for locals, and you can't get much more local than this legend, as you will soon learn.

Whaley House

Thomas Whaley might be behind one of the
most haunted houses in America, known as
the Whaley House. Some early brochures that
tried to promote San Diego to visitors said US
Congress officially gave the house a certificate
that calls it one of the most haunted places in
the country. It looks pretty boring from the
outside—it's a regular two-story house made

of wood and brick like a lot of other homes you might even see in your neighborhood. But inside is a different story.

Let's start at the beginning: the Whaley family has had a large part in American history: Thomas's grandfather worked with George Washington during the American Revolution! The family went on to create their own business developing tools for engineers. Thomas' father died when Thomas was a young boy and eventually Thomas took over the family business, though he didn't do so for very long. Thomas soon met a man who worked building ships. The man wanted Thomas's help in California, right around the time of the historic Gold Rush in 1849. Thomas traveled to San Francisco. Here, he had a store where he sold his own goods and those of the ship building company. But, after a fire destroyed the first home he built in San Francisco,

Thomas decided he had enough of the city and moved south—to San Diego.

After opening more stores with a business partner, Thomas had enough money to build a new home. It was around this same time he also married his grade school sweetheart, Anna, and the two welcomed several children together. Scarily, the cries of their babies were often drowned out by the strange sounds of boot stomping in their home. And Anna would often feel the presence of someone watching her even when she was totally alone.

There's a big reason why. You see, Thomas built his house on the grounds of a very tragic death of a man named "Yankee" Jim Robinson. This time around the California Gold Rush was a dangerous one. Not only were Native American tribes trying to save their land, but new settlers and explorers were also competing to make their riches, with many either dying in battle or being sentenced to death after going through trials in court.

The case of "Yankee" Jim was a particularly sad and gruesome one. Jim was a Canadian who, like many others, traveled to California at this time to literally strike gold. But Jim was a troublemaker and there was a rumor that he may have stalked and murdered coal miners to steal their possessions—though no one could ever prove it. Still, it gave him a bad reputation. But there was one event that did happen that would lead to Jim's sad ending.

One fateful night, he and two friends had too much to drink and stole a rowboat. Though it was a bad decision, the boat was unharmed and eventually the owners found it abandoned a few days later. But of course, Jim and his friends were later arrested and had to go to court to face a jury who would decide their fate. The owners of the boat were on his jury—which wasn't really fair—and as you can imagine, they gave him the worst punishment possible. They sentenced Jim to death by hanging.

On the date of his death, September 18, 1852, a lot of people gathered to watch it in the town square. One of them being Thomas Whaley. It was not a peaceful ending and seeing it really shook-up Thomas—so it's anyone's guess why he'd want to build his and Anna's house on those very grounds. In fact, the structure where "Yankee" Jim was hanged became an archway in the house! So, naturally, strange things started happening inside as Thomas, Anna and their children tried to sleep at night.

Not only that, but a couple of mysterious deaths happened here later, including a young friend of the family's children, named

Annabelle, who was said to have been strangled by a clothesline as the kids were playing outside in the yard. And then there was the death of the Whaley's young son Tommy Jr. before he was even two-years-old from a disease known as scarlet fever.

The devastated family moved to San Francisco for a bit to get away from the sadness in the house. They rented it out to a theater performer, Thomas Tanner, who built a stage in the living room and dining room and lived in the house with his actors. This actually made the Whaley House the first true theater in San Diego.

After some time, the Whaleys and their four children moved back and shared the house with the theater group. But just days after returning, Thomas Tanner suddenly died in the house even though he was neither sick nor old. His death was never explained. Some years later, the Whaleys' daughter Violet took her own life—and by then Thomas and Anna had enough of the house that they were convinced was cursed.

The house over time would have different families or businesses renting it, but eventually it sat vacant for some time. Today it's a museum that people can still visit. But those who do usually never return, as they feel very uneasy being inside the building. Some have reported feeling like they were being watched by a presence on the staircase and others said they were even pushed while on those stairs! Thankfully no one has been hurt. No one is really sure if this presence is "Yankee" Jim or perhaps the theater man Thomas Tanner.

But still others will hear a baby crying when they are in the upstairs of the Whaley House, where the family's nursery once was—this spirit is thought to be little Tommy Jr. Those who have taken pictures in this room can even see images of a ghostly baby when they look close.

Another area known for haunted activity is in the rooms that now have a replica of Thomas Tanner's theater stage. Some will see shadows moving on stage or even hear voices talking—maybe they're still rehearsing and wanting to put on a show? After all, as they say in theater, the show never ends.

The outside is another place for strange activity. Sometimes people swear they can see tragic little Annabelle still playing while others claim they see Anna Whaley in her gardens. She's also been known to haunt inside too, often seen in the bedroom overlooking the gardens where she died when she was 81 years old. Sometimes, when visitors come, they also claim to be greeted by a woman in old-fashioned clothing that they assume is an actor meant to look like the Whaley family living there at the time—but she knows a little *too* much about the house and family. Could they be talking to the real Anna?

Thomas Whaley also still "lives" in his beloved home, showing his presence with the strong smell of cigar smoke. There's no smoking allowed in the building so it's a "dead" giveaway when the scent comes up that Thomas is nearby, still making sure people know the Whaley behind the name of this very haunted house.

William Heath Davis House

There are a few key people in the history of San Diego—including William Heath Davis, who helped create the city as we know it today. You see, William was a very smart businessman and one of the wealthiest men in California for a long time. When he first came to visit San Diego in 1850, traveling from his home in San Francisco, he saw a big opportunity.

Most of San Diego at that time had been focused on Old Town, which was in the center of town and far away from the coast. But if you've ever visited a city by the ocean, you know how beautiful it is to look out at the scenic water. William imagined this for San Diego, too. What he envisioned was called "New Town," in the newer part of town he was developing.

As he set up and got started, William knew he needed a house for his family, which included his wife, Maria. She was part of the famous Estudillo family whose Casa was

featured in an earlier chapter of this book. The couple's house was in a part of town called the Gaslamp District where there were lots of entertainment venues like theaters. The Davis' house remains the oldest one to exist in New Town and it was one of a few William had arranged to be built and shipped over from the East Coast. He thought having these houses ready for families would encourage people to move to this new part of town—but sadly it was the opposite.

A lot of people from Old Town were against the idea and, even though California was in the middle of the historic Gold Rush, many were poor. William's idea failed and New Town soon became known as "Rabbitville" as more rabbits lived here than people! Sadly, William gave up on the idea and he never got to live in his house before leaving town.

Another important figure then came in to

take over. His name was Alonzo Horton, and he was another businessman who was able to build that dream city William had imagined but was not able to finish. Strangely enough, Alonzo moved into William's house while he was working on the project, but he was just one of the residents over the years. The house was also used as a hospital for San Diego residents for a while and even once was the hideout for a German spy in World War I!

Today, it's the Gaslamp Museum where people can visit and see a piece of San Diego history. A team redid the whole house to make each room look just like it did from different times in its long history. With so many lives lived and died in the house (it was a hospital after all!), it's said that not everyone has left the building.

There are things that happen here that

sound like they're straight out of a scary movie. Sometimes during a group tour the lights will go out as the group enters a room and then go back on when they leave. It's like the ghosts want them to stay out! And sometimes when those who work at the museum turn the lights off to go home for the day, they'll find them strangely back on when they arrive the next morning.

The "hospital room" is one that many people don't like going into—they say they can feel bad energy inside as well as cold air coming from one of the walls of the room. There's also a box here that has old medicine bottles like those that might have been used to treat patients back in the day. Though it's supposed to always be open, sometimes staff will find it closed and the bottles rearranged even though no one touched it.

In the dining room, sometimes the old-fashioned table settings look like they've been used too, with plates moved around and silverware where it shouldn't be. All that's really missing are food crumbs to make you believe a dinner party happened after hours.

One of the most eerie things seen in the William Heath Davis House though is the image of a woman who looks to have lived in the late 1800s. She can sometimes be seen leading people upstairs. Tour guests of the museum have often thought she is their guide and have followed her, but when the real tour guide looks for her, she can't be found. When this woman does appear, she's often near a spot called the "child's room" and some think it might be a mother who lost her child here, perhaps during a hospital stay. As some say, a mother never leaves her child's side, even in death.

CHAPTER 8

Horton Grand Hotel

If you ever thought it might be fun to have a sleepover with a ghost, you might want to visit the Horton Grand Hotel. If the name sounds familiar, you might remember the story of Alonzo Horton we talked about in the last story—he's one of the founding fathers of San Diego who helped build a busy center near its ocean coast, and this building honors him.

Alonzo made his money from selling supplies to coal miners, and later selling furniture. And he put a lot of that money into developing San Diego into a city people from all over the world would want to visit. And that of course meant the city needed hotels for them to stay in.

In 1886, the Grand Hotel was opened near where the ships and trains let people off into town. It had an Eastern European look, with beautiful wood carvings, large windows, and etched stone. Because of its beauty, it gave off a rich feeling and people who had a good amount of money often stayed here, even former US president Benjamin Harrison.

Around the same time, there was another hotel being built in this part of town called the Brooklyn Hotel, which attracted the opposite kind of character—a lot of cowboys and gamblers. One of them was the famous

Wyatt Earp who was a Western frontier man who tried to take the law into his own hands and was also a very good gambler. He and his wife Josie opened several saloons and gambling halls in San Diego, and they lived in the Brooklyn Hotel for about seven years, from 1890 to around 1897.

But, as the years went on and newer hotels were built, both the Grand Hotel and the Brooklyn Hotel were in danger of being torn down and forgotten about forever. A group of people came together to save them, carefully taking apart and then combining the two buildings in a new spot. Now joined together, the property has been renamed the Horton Grand Hotel and its history has traveled with it—including many of the spirits of people that used to book rooms.

One of the most frequent ghosts is a man named Roger Whitaker. In the late 1800s,

Roger booked Room 309 at the Brooklyn and went off to play some card games at the gambling hall in town. But he got into trouble. You see, Roger was cheating the other players during a game of poker, and they soon caught on to it. One of them pulled a gun out of his pocket, which sent Roger running all the way back to his room at the Brooklyn. But the men followed him, knocked down the door to the room and eventually found Roger hiding in the big wardrobe closet where they shot him dead.

Roger never really left Room 309 where overnight guests can still feel his presence. Sometimes the lights flicker out of control,

 things will strangely move around in the bathroom right in front of people's eyes or the bed will shake like a demon is awaking guests from their sleep. And it's said if you leave some playing cards out,

they will be rearranged in the morning like someone had played with them—sometimes the staff can even hear cards being shuffled when no one has booked the room!

The famous Wyatt Earp also likes to play with cards that are left out, usually tricking guests in Room 209. If the cards are a losing mix, they will be placed down by morning when guests wake up. So, if you ever stay here, you'll want to play those cards right or risk meeting one of these gambling men.

The *Star of India*

The *Star of India*

Water is said to be a way that the energy of ghosts can travel, so you can imagine that San Diego has many spirits that haunt near its coastline. That includes many of the historic ships that were once used by the Navy and for early trading, though today they serve as museums. One of them is called the *Star of India*, as that was often where this sailing ship headed to pick up spices and other goods.

Because of the many tragedies that happened on board, some consider it a cursed ship. In its first voyage out of England in 1863, it was struck by another ship and suffered a lot of damage. After being repaired, it tried to set sail again but this time it was damaged again by a large storm. Its captain, William Story, got very sick and died on board. He was given a burial at sea and many of his crewmen refused to be part of any mission on the ship again after all the bad experiences.

It was then sold a couple of times, with the various owners setting it on sail across the world, to New Zealand, Hawaii and the nearby Pacific Islands, Australia and even Alaska, which brought the large vessel to the US. For several years until 1923, it would go back and forth between Alaska and San Francisco, transporting coal, fishermen, and salmon. But as steamboats became more convenient than sailboats, the *Star of India* fell out of service. It was tied up at shore for a very long time.

Finally, in 1976—thanks to a group of people who raised enough money to repair it and get it working again—the ship went out to sea. Still working today, it's the oldest sailing vessel of its kind still making regular trips. They're mostly short trips, though. The *Star of India* is used for a lot of overnight trips for children to learn about sailing. Likely, these kids have met another child while on board— the ghost of little John Campbell whose story also helps give the *Star of India* its reputation for being cursed.

Though the year is not totally clear, at one point John was a runaway who was found by the crew living on board. But rather than kick him off, the captain at the time decided to let him stay and train him to be part of the crew. Even though he was young, everyone on board really liked him, which makes his story even sadder. One day, John was climbing up one of the sails, but he slipped and fell a long way down to the ship's deck. He was bedridden for three days, where many of the crew took turns staying by his side, but John eventually passed away from his injuries. John still loves being on the ship though, and is very friendly with those now on board—perhaps too friendly! Whether he's laughing right into your ear or grabbing your hand and swinging your arm, he likes to make an appearance. He often appears in photos, too.

Another weird thing that happens today is that people can smell food cooking, even though none of the ovens have worked or been turned on in years. This happens so often that the museum staff call it the ship's "ghost cook." Whoever it is really loves making food as they can be heard clinking pots and pans and swinging soup ladles on kitchen hooks even though no human is there to make all that racket.

There's also a part of the *Star of India* where the captain's area, doctor's office, and dining room are all located. This is where old Captain Story (who died on the first voyage) is often seen staring at maps as if he's still trying to steer the ship on its journeys. Near the doctor's office, voices can be heard comforting each other, likely some of the crewmen stuck in time trying to comfort sick and injured sailors.

One of the men who died on board also haunts belowdecks near where the anchor is stored. One day when the sailor was doing repairs, the ship started moving while he was down there. He screamed an yelled to get the attention of the other sailors, but they couldn't hear him. As the enormous anchor and chain were pulled up from the seabed, they pinned the poor sailor and eventually crushed him. When he didn't report for duty later on, the crew thought he had run away. His body was found days later. Visitors today can hear moans and screams in this area and feel very cold walking near it, likely from the spirit of this man who gave his life to be part of the ship's history.

CHAPTER
10

Steamship *Berkeley*

Ships of all shapes and sizes have docked near San Diego's ocean coastline, but there are not many as impressive as the Steamship *Berkeley*. It was once one of the country's largest ferries—a massive vessel that could carry even cars aboard—and it would make regular trips from Oakland to San Francisco carrying up to 1,700 workers and travelers back and forth around all the water ways of the Bay Area.

In fact, the Steamship *Berkeley* had an important part in history. In 1906, about eight years after its first voyage, the Great San Francisco Earthquake happened that also sparked a large fire, and it left lots of destruction and people needing to urgently leave the city. The *Berkeley* was a lifesaver, transporting thousands of people to safety and carrying supplies and more emergency workers to help with the disaster.

After this time, as more families purchased cars, ferries weren't needed as much to transport people. And so, the *Berkeley* stopped its regular service. It was sold and spent some time as a gift shop at sea before the San Diego Maritime Museum purchased the ship and made it beautiful again—it's now even a National Historic Landmark. Today, people can visit on board and see what it used to look like a century ago, and even get a close look at the large steam engine that powered it. The *Berkeley* is often used for weddings and large events and for research for scientists— and ghost hunters, too. The ship is incredibly haunted, and there's one man who seems to be behind it all. He's known as "the Fedora Man" for the old-fashioned hat he's always seen wearing. His real name though is likely John O. Norbom—he's the only man who is known to have passed away while on the ship.

In January 1911, John was seen walking the upper decks of the *Berkeley* with a strange bottle in his hands. Inside, it contained a liquid explosive that is used to make dynamite. As he put the bottle in his back pocket, a door to one of the cabins swung open and hit him in just the right spot that it set off the materials into a small explosion. It's said John went flying into the ceiling and crashed to the lower deck. He died from his injuries. Five other people were injured but survived. No one is sure why John was carrying the liquid, but some think he may have purposely taken his life. Whatever the reason, he's clearly not at peace. Visitors today will sometimes feel doors slam shut behind them with a ton of force and sometimes the doors will lock with no explanation.

There may also be a little girl on board who's not part of our world. When a few ghost hunters have brought equipment on the ship to record voices, they have captured a child asking for her mommy. The voice has come from the lower part of the ship were the crew live, which is strange, since no official records show a crew member who had a young daughter.

Other strange occurrences include items and tools that go missing, the sound of footsteps or even whispered talking when no guests are on board. With all the voyages this incredible ship took, it's no surprise that not everyone has left yet.

USS *Midway*

CHAPTER 11

USS *Midway*

Every year, thousands of people walk along the decks of the USS *Midway*—but not all of them are living. Some are former sailors that want to relive life at sea, and others are wandering spirits who just want to see the ship in all its glory. The USS *Midway* is well known as one of the most majestic ships used during a number of wars in the 20th Century. And, until 1955, it was considered the largest ship ever built in America!

It could hold large numbers of troops and weapons and was a great benefit to America during wartime. It was first meant to be used during World War II, but was wasn't fully built until right before the war ended. However, it was later used in the Vietnam War and then, decades later, in Desert Storm in the Middle East. In total, it has traveled all the world's oceans, spent more than forty years as part of America's Navy, and has won many awards.

The USS *Midway* also had many tragedies as well—battles are never won easily and, sadly, many people lost their lives on the ship. In February 1948, off the coast of France, one of the USS

Midway's smaller boats overturned and sent eight crewmen into the icy waters below, killing them. There was also a collision in 1954 due to high waves while the ship was near Greece, an event that took the lives of an additional eight men. And in 1990 two back-to-back explosions caused a fire that killed three firemen and hurt eight crewmen (eight seems to be a bad number for this ship, doesn't it?).

Altogether, it's believed more than 100,000 crewmen have lived and worked on this ship. Even though many have passed away, they still come "home" to the USS *Midway*, which is now a museum docked in San Diego. It's believed that many of the former Navy sailors are the ghosts that haunt the USS *Midway*. There are about thirty of them for sure and some make their presence known by overtaking the mannequins on the ship, making them come to life! Some visitors swear that these doll-like figures (resembling the people that once served on the ship) have talked to them and told them history. But in fact, only one of the dozens of mannequins has a recorded voice so there's no explanation for the others.

The area known as the "sick bay" (a hospital on board) is where museum visitors often feel uncomfortable. They might become dizzy or feel like they are going to be sick, or just have a very bad feeling and leave the area immediately. And as soon as they do, they are magically better. This makes sense since the sick bay is where service men wounded in battle would come to be treated and many likely died here, too, leaving behind spirits that are not at rest.

Point Loma Lighthouse

Point Loma Lighthouse

Is there anything more eerie than an abandoned lighthouse that spreads a beacon of illumination across foggy waters? With its bright light shining into the distance, it can almost feel like spirits are walking across the water—and in the case of Point Loma Lighthouse, maybe they are. Located on the western part of San Diego Harbor, it was one of the first lighthouses ever built on California's massive shoreline and it was also one of the tallest ever.

But that presented a big problem. Because it was so tall (422 feet above sea level!), when low hanging clouds and fog came in off the water, the light it beamed out was almost completely blocked making the lighthouse rather useless.

Lighthouse keepers would have to stay up all night using whistles and horns to warn ships away. Finally, after a few decades since it first shone bright in 1855, the lighthouse was taken out of service in 1891.

A new, much shorter, lighthouse was built closer to the shoreline. Now the light could shine for twenty-five miles and not be blocked by clouds and fog. However, the old Point Loma Lighthouse remained, though it was abandoned. Without regular care and maintenance it began to fall apart. Former president Woodrow Wilson paid a visit in 1913 and declared the site a historic natural park, which it remains today. The lighthouse itself is

only ever open two days a year, August 25 (the national park's birthday) and November 15 (the day Point Loma was first lit)—but there's still a lot of activity every day of the year.

When people do visit, they might run into Robert D. Israel and his family. Robert was one of the many lighthouse keepers that ran the old Point Loma for eighteen years when it was still fully functioning. His wife and family lived there too—often joining people for picnics on the surrounding land. His kids even had to row a boat across the bay to get to school.

Of course, Robert is no longer alive, but it's said his spirit still lingers in the nooks and crannies of this old building. Sometimes visitors will hear footsteps coming from the upstairs and on the long spiral staircase that reaches up to the watchtower. Some have even said they could feel heavy breathing behind their ears when no one was around. Still others have said they feel like they are being watched or feel cold spots in certain areas of the lighthouse, and a few have claimed to see Robert's actual ghost. It may be he's never really left work and doesn't seem to want to retire anytime soon!

The Hotel del Coronado

Coronado Island in San Diego Bay is a fabulous stretch of land surrounded by beaches and sunny weather that has been a favorite vacation spot of the rich and famous for over one hundred years. Coronado, in fact, translates to "crown" in Spanish.

With so many interesting people who have visited the island—and so many others who have wanted to—there's lots of unsettled energy here. Ghostly things happen every day, especially at the Hotel del Coronado.

Built right before the 1900s, this beautiful building has all the bells and whistles—with big chandeliers, impressive woodcarvings, and large staircases. When it first opened, this incredible resort attracted wealthy people, especially in the winters when they wanted to get away from the cold. The Hotel del Coronado offered beaches, pools, music, dancing, and a large golf course. It was also one of the first hotels to have an elevator, electricity, and telephones.

Although not all the visitors had such fortunate lives. One guest by the name of Kate Morgan is perhaps the saddest story to come out of Hotel del Coronado. When she arrived on Thanksgiving Day 1892, not much was known about her. In fact she used a fake name when checking in to Room 302—Lottie

A. Bernard—and said she was from Detroit, but that was also not true.

Kate acted very strangely according to the hotel staff. First, she had no baggage, which was odd for someone coming to the property. And she seemed very ill—every day she stayed at the hotel, she'd wander down to the drugstore and ask for some new medicine to try to cure her, claiming she had an illness that made her body have bad pains and stomachaches (she later told one of the hotel workers that she had stomach cancer). When the staff tried to call a doctor for her, she would refuse. She always said her brother, Dr. Anderson, would be coming from Indianapolis to join her soon and cure her. Every day she asked the front desk if he had checked in, and every day it was the same answer: no. This only made her sadder and weaker.

One day she took a train into the town of San Diego, which is a little ways from Coronado Island, saying she had to try to get her baggage from the station. But instead, Kate went to a gun shop and bought a pistol that she said was a gift for someone. When she returned to the hotel that night, that was the last time she was seen alive. The next morning her body was found with that same gun next to it. No one at the hotel ever heard a gunshot but, regardless, Kate was dead.

Much was discovered about her after she died—that her name was Kate Morgan (not Lottie), she was from Omaha, her parents were long gone, and she was raised by her grandfather. Most recently she was unhappily married to a man named Thomas. She left him and began working as a maid for a family in California but left suddenly that fateful Thanksgiving. By all accounts, Kate seemed to be a very sad woman though she wasn't sick. When her body was examined, no cancer was found. But everything else—like why she came to the hotel, who her brother was, why she seemed so frail—is still a mystery. It almost seems like Kate wants people to solve it since she keeps hanging around the hotel today.

So many have seen her that the hotel now captures all the guest stories in a book. One guest in the '90s claimed that, while staying in Room 3327 (the new Room 302 after some remodeling), the lights would flicker on and off. And there was a time she reached for a new bath towel except it had someone else's lipstick all over it. If she tried to use the phone, she would hear only static, and the keycard to her room never worked properly.

Other guests have said they have heard a woman sobbing while they were trying to sleep and believed it to be Kate. Some have also said their phones got messages from Room 3327 and other times the TV in the room would turn off and on for no reason.

One man who booked Kate's room on three different occasions during business trips would encounter several weird things like the phone ringing with no one on the other end of the line, lights going on and off, and towels ending up in the bathtub even though he knew he didn't put them there. One time he told Kate to "knock it off" and instead of the strange things stopping, a loud alarm clock went off. On the third trip, when the man's wife came with him, they found a bouquet of roses outside their door with no note—they still have no idea how it got there.

A couple that booked a stay at Hotel del Coronado one Valentine's Day weekend had a very interesting experience, too. They had no idea about the haunting but that night as they were sleeping in Room 3327, the man witnessed the blanket covers being pulled back from him. It startled him and as he woke up to see what was going on, he saw a woman standing at the foot of his bed tugging at the blankets. Once he spotted her, she vanished. But then the doorknob to the room start rattling unexpectedly, like she was trying to get back in.

Another scary incident happened about twenty years ago, when curious guests wanted to see Kate's room. When a hotel worker brought them there, they saw an imprint of a woman's body in the bed. It looked like someone had slept in it. But the room was unoccupied; it been cleaned and was awaiting a new guest. The hotel worker tried to smooth out the bedspread but the shape of the body kept coming back. The guests were so freaked out they ran from the room.

Hauntings have happened in other rooms too—one time when former president George Bush visited, one of his secret service agents complained to the front desk of loud footsteps and noises coming from the room above him. He asked staff if they could talk to the guests so they would quiet down. The only problem was, there was no room above his. Another time, in Room 3517 two guests awoke early in the morning after hearing a voice tell them in their ear to go to the window. When they did they saw a beautiful sunrise. Each woman thanked the other for letting her know about it—but neither one had spoken a word that morning!

And that's not even counting all the unexplained things that happen in the gift shops and on the outside grounds.

Conclusion

Now that you've read about the many spooky stories in San Diego—from the most haunted house in America: the Whaley House, to the story of sad Kate Morgan at the Hotel del Coronado—you can see why it's considered one of the most haunted places in the country. So even though it looks sunny and peaceful, you secretly know what lies beyond the surface and you can be on the lookout for when you visit, if you dare!

Selena Fragassi is a Chicago-based writer who grew up in a real haunted house and has loved all things paranormal since she had her first experience with a ghost as a teenager. In addition to writing for Spooky America, Selena is a music journalist and has written for such publications as the *Chicago Sun-Times*, *Chicago Tribune*, A.V. Club, Blurt, Paste, Popmatters, Under The Radar, and Nylon, among others. She is also working on an upcoming novel about her grandfathers' experiences during World War II.

Check out some of the other Spooky America titles available now!

Spooky America was adapted from the creeptastic Haunted America series for adults. Haunted America explores historical haunts in cities and regions across America. Each book chronicles both the widely known and less-familiar history behind local ghosts and other unexplained mysteries. Here's more from *Haunted Heart of San Diego* author Brian Clune: